Walter Norton Evans

Mount Royal

Walter Norton Evans

Mount Royal

ISBN/EAN: 9783337317829

Printed in Europe, USA, Canada, Australia, Japan

Cover: Foto ©Andreas Hilbeck / pixelio.de

More available books at **www.hansebooks.com**

Mount Royal

by

WALTER NORTON EVANS.

ILLUSTRATED

BY

ELIZABETH WARREN AND A.B. CLARKSON

The Poet
approaches the
mountain in
YOUTH.

Hail, Royal Mountain!
                    Venerable pile!
Gray-headed sentinel from that far past
When the creative fiat erst went forth,
And the dry land appeared above the main.
Loud roar'd the seas; the floods did clap
        their hands;
When from the waters thou didst lift thy head,
Rearing it towards the azure dome above,
There to be bathed in the pure light of God.

As thou didst stand alone,
                    amid the waste
Of many waters, searching sky above
And sea below, didst thou not feel the thrill
Of the Almighty Spirit moving o'er thee,
Within thee, and around?
                    Did He not speak to thee?
Well hast thou kept His secret thro' the ages:
And in thy rocky heart we read to-day,
How thou the mighty fiat didst obey.

Thou patriarch of hills - so old, yet young
    And fresh to-day, by thine obedience
To the same mighty law which gave thee birth,
Take me within thy wide-embracing arms,
And, while I rest upon thy grassy lap,
Tell me, thy lover, ever fond and true,
The secret thou hast cherished for so long.

8

The Mountain
replies by pointing
to
THE SUNRISE.

Dost thou see the golden glory,
  Waking in the dreamy east;
Tingeing all the mountain summits,
  Clothed in grey and heavy mist?
    Wave on wave of light is breaking;
      Morning breezes gently play;
    And, in brightness none can gaze on,
      Rises now the orb of day.

Nearer, rolls the quiet river
        Ever onward toward the sea:
Dark and sullen are its waters,
        Till the daybreak silently
Beams upon them. — warmer tintings
        Blend upon its bosom cold;
And the magic of the morning
        Changes all to burnish'd gold.
Onward, through the sparkling ether,
        Comes the lusty morning breeze,

Steals the perfume from the hay-mows;
    Rustles now among the trees :-
Birds pour forth their liquid music;
    Squirrels chatter loud and long;
Insects, soaring, creeping, crawling,
    Join to swell the matin song.
Morning in the silent mountain ;-
    Morning in the balmy air ;-
Morning in the happy valley :-
    Glowing morning everywhere.

Change on change, thro' countless ages,
    Has been wrought by unseen hand;
Mighty waves of ocean rolling
        Where lies now the fruitful land.
Torrid heat has bathed my summit,
        Clothing me with herbage rare;-
And, anon, eternal winter
        Spread his empire everywhere.

11

Then the Ice-King, grim and silent,
    Glistening armies forward led,
All subduing; and the fallen
    Grinding 'neath his flinty tread.
Change on change, through countless ages;
    Still the miracle of day
Never yet has failed in breaking;
    Never halted on its way.

Faintly, like a distant echo
        From the long-forgotten years;
Nearer roll the strong vibrations,
        Thundering now in mortal ears:-
Never, while the earth remaineth,
        Shall the ordered seasons fail:

"Day shall wake to brave endeavour;
    "Night shall spread its restful veil.
  "Hope shall tint youth's early morning;
    "Love, light manhood's cloudy way;
  "And old age's rapid current,
      "Faith shall gild with endless day."

18

Weary with the cares of life, and depressed by its shams and disappointments, the Poet approaches the mountain in

MANHOOD.

Weary world of
        disappointed hope,
Of thwarted aims,
              and pitiful defeats.
    Successes,
              worse than failures, lifting up
Their gilded victims to a giddy height,
  Only to cast them to a lower hell.
The golden lever in unskilled hands.
Unlovely hearts, whose sympathies have turned
  To gall and wormwood,
                made the poison'd channels
Through which the sweetest ministries of life
Shall be poured forth upon the pure white souls
  That do and bear, and bless humanity.

A golden calf set in the market-place;
    And worshippers, in bloody sacrifice,
Off'ring what should be dearest:—
        character,
Honour and heart, upon the reeking
            altar.

    How many a noble soul, that started forth
    On life's great voyage, with a fav'ring gale,
    Drawn from its course by unexpected tides,
    Like a tall ship involv'd in dangerous shoals,
    Ambition fills the sail; Greed takes the helm,
    And the proud ship of Manhood lies a wreck
    Upon the sharp and flinty rock of Self.

Where shall I hide me
from the mournful sight?
Where shall I rest my weary, aching head:
And cool my feverish lips?
To Horebs brow
The care-worn leader of the desert host
Withdrew, that he might be alone with God:

And there, in earnest, consecrated thought.
  He heard th'inspiring voice of Deity,
And gazed upon Jehovah face to face.
  Oh! Royal Mountain!

                    Holy Mount to me.
I come to thee, as in bright days of yore:
  That by thy pure and calming ministry,
In reverence and deep humility,
  I may be brought nearer the heart of God,
And hear His voice in Nature's voice around

NOON.

The Mountain soothes the
Poet by the simple sights and
sounds of Nature about him;
then points to the river as a
striking and hopeful emblem
of life.

Here on the smooth
and elastic turf,
Where the grass is growing
fresh and green;
Where the
ox-eyed daisies
gracefully bend,
And the golden
buttercups peep between;
Where the sumach fans with her feathery hands,
And the maple gives a grateful shade;
Where we hear the song of the summer wind,
As it tenderly woos the shadowy glade;—
Here soothe the nerves, and rest the brain,
And trust and comfort will come again.

See yon little bird,
        in her mossy nest,
Pressing close,
        With her downy   breast
        Three tiny eggs and   joyfully
Eyeing her mate, who on yonder tree
        Warbles his song so rejoicingly.
Dear little birds! Do they fume and fret
        About the seasons, dry or wet?
Do they worry about the winter to come,
That shall drive them away
                        from their Northern home?
No :- They do their duty, and sing their song,
    And trust in Providence all day long.

Nature has many
        a delicate
                tone
We hear not, because
        of our hurrying feet;
Yet we miss, when the
        exquisite note is gone,
The   harmony,
        tender and sweet.
'T is only a melody sharp and clear,
That fills with delight
        the untrain'd ear;
While the subtle harmonies
        echo find
        In the calm retreats
        of the cultured mind.

Are you rested yet?
                Then quietly stroll
        To yonder smooth and grassy knoll.
Away to the south the river is seen,
                Embosom'd soft in living green;
Its calm, blue waters, clear and bright,
Seem dancing now with a childs delight,
                And with the sunbeams play.
But soon, with youth's impetuous stride
They seem the lazy bank to chide
                And, laughing, roll away.

On, still on, with
increasing strife,
They enter on
the battle of life;
Forward they pour
With a mighty roar;
And the white foam flies,
and hisses,
and falls;
And wave to wave
in thunder calls.
The firm rocks quake, as the waters pass
Over their sides, a seething mass.
Anon they gather their frenzied force
For a mighty leap on their headlong course:—
The iron-bound rocks
are split asunder,
As with a voice like distant thunder,
Roaring and hissing, down they go,
Into the boiling cauldron below.

Exhausted, the waters linger awhile,
Calm and cool, round the Holy Isle:

And they widen their bounds,
                        and learn at length
To use for others their mighty strength.
Past the crowded city they flow,
Bearing a blessing to high and low:—
They ripple round islands verdure-drest,
Calm as the islands of the blest:—

Cardinal flowers deck the water's edge,
And wild-ducks hide in the leafy sedge.
Onward they press with majestic motion;—
  The shores recede, and the waters wide
  The impulse feel of an inward tide
That rolls as a welcome from the ocean:—
  As the Spirit comes to the striving soul,
  A welcome guide to the longed-for goal.

32

And far away, with calm delight,
 The river with the ocean blends;
Leaving no trace, to mortal sight,
 Where ocean rolls, and river ends:-
As the soul no severing mark will see
When time blends into eternity.

Gaze on the azure dome above,
Bending o'er all, like a Father's love.
Its arches far and wide are spread
From the glowing centre above your head;
Telling that sympathy and care
Are with us here and everywhere;
And o'er the hearts that sadly pine,
Is the central spring of aid divine.

34

Sleep, weary labourer!
        Rest is sweet
'Neath the pine-trees' shade,
    in the noontide heat.
The gentle fanning of summer air
Shall sooth the
    fevered brow
of care.
    The drowsy hum of the honey bee
    Shall be a lullaby sweet to thee.
Birds shall sing in thy dreaming ears,
    And flowers their perfume shed;
And happy visions of by-gone years
    Shall soothe thine aching head.

Wake, rested labourer! Hope returns:—
A brighter vision within thee burns.
Nature's lessons of truth and beauty
Are trumpet calls to earnest duty.
Not what we have had, but what we are,
Shall measure us at the judgment bar.
There is little need for the anxious thought,
    If the loving heart be thine;
And the seed that is sown with the brave "I ought,"
    Will bring forth fruit divine.

The Poet
approaches the
mountain in
OLD AGE.

Once more,
old friend,
with weary steps
and slow,
I come
to mount thy
venerable sides,
To gaze upon
the wide
expanded view;

To drink in
the enchantment of the scene;
To waken tend'rer views of human life;
To hold communion with th'Eternal Spirit.
Here, in the days of youth, I watch'd the dawn
Spreading her golden mantle all around,
Revealing beauties lying unsuspect,
And Nature vocal with the voice of God.

Ah! Golden Youth!
                From me are gone for aye
My halcyon days; yet thou'rt perpetual.
And now, reclining at the tireless feet
Of children's children, I can voice the lesson
That thou, in by-gone days, hast taught to me.
Thrice blest the youth, who, from his mother's
        knee,
Where he has learned to lisp the praise of God,

Turns to the open book of God Himself,
To find revealed the thoughts that He
has thought.

To him, how poor the wretched syren-voice
Of selfishness and sin:— it woos in vain.

Through many a bower of living green I pass;
  By many a glade, whose daisy-dotted sward
Elastic springs beneath my trembling feet,

Bringing sensations of an earlier day:—
On to the mountain summit, where I lay
In strong and loving angel arms, and heard
Through Nature's voice, which is the voice
        of God,
Lessons of courage, confidence, and peace.
Here as I lie beneath the maple shade,
How glorious a view is spread for me.

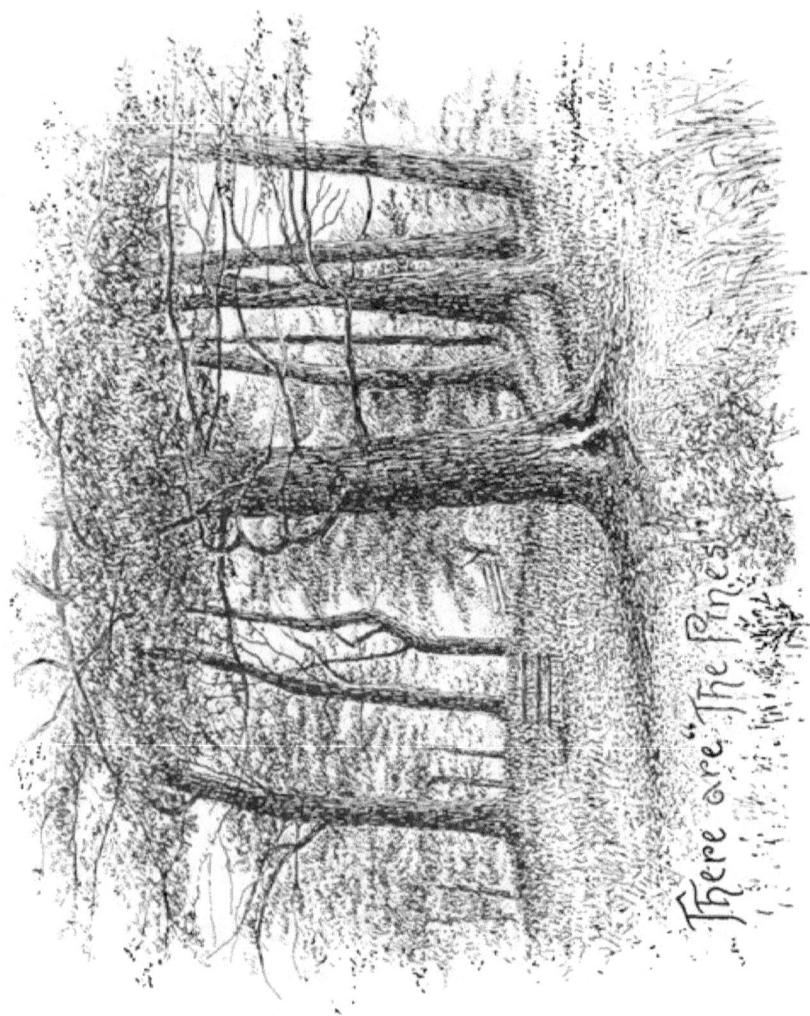

There are "The Pines"

Where many a wild halloo
On moonlight nights in winter, has aroused
The sleeping echoes;

when the
snow-shoers,

In blanket suit, with brightly coloured sash,
And tuque of red or blue; their mocassins
Of moose-skin, smoothly drawn on well-
    sock'd foot,
And snow-shoe firmly bound with deer-skin
    thong,
Wound up the hill in long extended files,
Singing and shouting with impetuous glee.

How glorious, when silent stars look down,

And pale moon
glistens on the
stainless snow;
And leafless branches blend in gothic arches

To make a fairy palace on the hills!
Beneath my feet, the winding mountain
    road;
Beyond, a gently rising ground, whereon
Dwarf oaks, and silver birch, and sugar
    maples,
With interlocking arms, are like good friends
Of varied mind and state, yet all unite

To bless each other,
   and to help mankind.
While yonder lie the hill and meadow-land,
Now emerald green, but on bright winter nights,
  Upon whose snowy bosom happy crowds
Fly on the swift toboggan down the hill,
  And o'er the broad expanse;

or toilsomely
Ascend the steep incline;
when fairy forms
Lean for support upon the stalwart arms;
Then listen, feigning doubt, but all believing,
To the firm accents of a manly voice
That speaks in true and earnest tones of love.
And now, thou subtle Spirit of the Mountain,
To whose enchanting voice I oft have listened;
Speak to me once again prophetic words
That shall give comfort to my weary heart,
And make mine age but as the bloom of youth.

The Spirit of the Mountain, directing the Poet's gaze across the "City of Silence," shows the heavenly gates open in THE SUNSET.

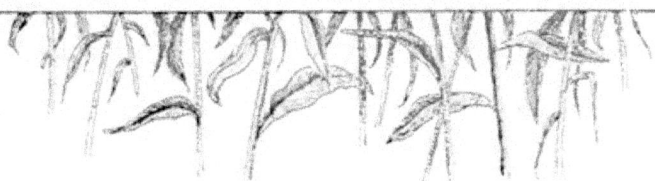

Child of the earth; thou whose spirit immortal
    Time and its changes can never control;
As thou approachest the grave's dismal portal,
    Sunlight eternal shall beam on thy soul.
Long hast thou loved o'er the mountain to wander;
    Each secret haunt to thy feet hast been known;
Every sweet lesson of love thou hast pondered,
    In bird or in wild-flower; in leaf or in stone —
        Prayerfully pondered it,
Earnestly striving to make it thine own.

Age may approach;
        but whoe'er on the mountain
    In the Veiled Presence has reverently trod,
He has drunk deep of the life-giving fountain
        Filled with the grand inspiration of God.
With awe he unravels the mystery of ages,
    And secrets divine are breathed into his ear;
As in wonder he searches the God-written pages,
    Unseen, yet impressive, the Author draws near;-
        Draws near so tenderly
Broad'ning his vision, dispelling his fear-

See below in the valley,
  Embosomed in trees,
O'er which wanders calmly
  The flower-scented breeze,
The "City of Silence";
  Whose monuments rise,
Like fingers prophetic
  That point to the skies.

To low wails of sorrow
    The echoes awake;
Or hearts hide their anguish,
    And silently break;

While Nature, kind mother,
    Broods over the tomb,
And decks its dim arches
    In beauty and bloom

But the valley, whose windings
    Are hid by our tears,
Opens broad on the mountains
    Of undying years:
And the soul that has listened
    To Nature's calm tone,
Hears the same voice of
        sweetness
From Heaven's high throne.

Oh! Erebus midnight
Preceding the morn:—
Oh! travail of anguish
That joy may be born.

Go patient endeavour.
The blessing is given:—
The faithful of earth are
The sainted of Heaven.

But not in graves the thought of man
      can rest;
Were that the end, life were, indeed, unblest.
Better to be the spring-reviving sod,
Than soul forbid to share the life of God.

Behold, beyond the "City of the Dead,"
How fair the landscape to our vision spread;
And in the midst the silent river lies,
Its calm, clear waters mirroring the skies:—

"Lake of two Mountains;"—not the Stygian stream
That darkly filled the ancient poet's dream:
But, like a soul that manfully has striven,
Blending with shades of earth the light of
    heaven.

And now the sun across the azure deep,
Moves to his setting with majestic sweep;
God's inspiration in the holy glow,
Fills the blue vault above, the earth below:-
Spirit to spirit calls:- in awe we kneel,
Th' uplifting of a Real Presence feel;
And there, encircled in a flood of light,
The Golden Gates beam on our raptured
    sight!

The Poet bids Farewell to the mountain.

Farewell. Old Mountain!
       From thy wood-crown'd heights
I bear away a deeper. dearer sense
Of "God-with-me" than e'er I knew before.
Mounts of Transfiguration still there are.
That lift us far above the influence
Of time and sense, and bring us nearer heaven:

And such thou art to me.—When in the valley
We feel our limitations, grieve, and fret;
And then, in wild despair, look to the hills;
For there are wisdom, strength, and boundless
    love.
Thou blessed mountain-teacher, fare-thee-well!